the
ornamental
world

poetry

retta
bowen

tall-lighthouse

for my parents

Acknowledgements: thanks to the editors and publishers of Magma, where some of these poems, or versions of these poems first appeared.

With thanks to Roddy Lumsden and Simon Armitage for invaluable advice and support, to Linda Chase and to Lois Rowe, and to the Society of Authors – much gratitude.

Epigraph taken from an untitled poem by *Tua Forsström* in her collection *The Snow Leopard* (Bloodaxe 1990)

cover image: mat redvers

cover photo: chloë barter

tall-lighthouse pilot publication - new poetry from young poets - series edited by Roddy Lumsden and supported by Arts Council England

ISBN 978-1-904551-44-7

tall-lighthouse
www.tall-lighthouse.co.uk

contents

We take place at unknown depths
in insufficient light, but even what
can be seen is beautiful.
Tua Forsström

To understand nothing finally

To understand nothing finally but the sly betrayals,
the way the body suffers indignities at rest
or responds to the lightest touch in sleep;
the way we mooch across the carpet in shoddy slippers
with a cup of tea, as though that tea might save us.

Last night I walked the tenements of every hour –
bedroom, toilet, kitchen, dammit – surprised
by the modicum of space, the frankness of fridge
                                                    and door
and the cold resorts; stood unnerved in makeshift lights,
then snapped them off to a scorch of dark.

Only in glimpses can we know what we are born for;
all morning the back door stands wide in alarm
on the ease of rain that is pardoning the garden,
the wind chimes jostling for their claim on sound.

The Mountain

When he comes down from the mountain
where he died, and hears the air is kind,
the breeze surging with birds
and the proceeds of breath refining the trees
to a stark green, he is at ease again.
He stands on a jut of rock and allows his hands
to unfurl on a thought: *I am no longer tired.*

He has visited the loneliness of gods,
watched the brief world collapse back
on itself, with the lake laid like a coin in the palm,
and the fields bent. He has shouted out
a flock of birds from the earth's highest point.
He has moved beyond himself
and is in summer; he will do nothing but see.

Here's a man

who is not at odds with tennis whites,
cricket whites or tux, or the old tunes
that crackle as he shifts from foot to foot
in a sway of need that pleased the ladies,

who knows the art of tipping, the sharp
quip, who knows if he goes too far
to jaunt back with a gift (unwrapped) -
aeroplane freebie, tacky T-shirt, TB,

who lugged a 40-foot boat across moors
with five men, slept in a ditch, jumped
or was pushed from a train, blew one frail
shell of his hearing clean out with a gun,

who from then on was deaf to doorbell,
alarm clock, telephone, or any demand,
would tug the soft flesh of his lobe with
a quizzical tilt like a game of charades,

who slept through books, meals, plays
(snored while his son was on stage),
his head knocked back to a startled gape
at the perennial blank snowfall of days,

who wears the face his mother gave him,
packed off at five like a miniature envoy
on the posting of a lifetime, equipped with
hockey stick, trunk, tuck-box and a tie

ready-noosed to save a struggle later; who,
all the sorry miles from Rajasthan to Wales,
to the alma mater waiting with her gates
thrown open, cried behind a newspaper,

who pitched up at their Christmas door
one year like a stray, begging to be let in,
blindly shouting he was sorry for whatever
he had done. They couldn't hear a thing.

Rivalries

I had a head start, being dead
at birth and brought back to life
or so, but you wear your hot scar
like a notch on the bedpost,
and we almost came to blows
over who'd suffered the most.

Some Days

i.m. Dorothy Jenkins

I think of you when I am quiet of mind,
late winter days, the aftermath of rain.
Days you'd buzz me in and I'd take the stairs
three at a time to the sound of your voice
from a high landing: *Is that you, Anne?*

Days when I was the wrong person
and the wrong height, dropping my knees
to the green rug to put my arms
round your waist, so as not to shame you,
in your heeled slippers, with a stooped hug.

Each time I hugged you the last time,
and touched the soft swatch of your hair,
astonished by sleep. The smell of calm
and talc rising from garments laid out
in the bedroom; the kettle always on.

We would stand at the French windows
and watch passers by, swishing to and fro
on the glistening roads, as boats at sea.
You never wanted me to leave. Some days
you come back to me, or I return to you.

Solstice

The time we first made love,
                    coins cascaded
through the glass-fronted till
                    of my childhood.
Wind thronged the brickwork
of a blue afternoon,
          the failed, saintly lights
of a Clapton solstice.

A tap had been left running
                    in another room.
You went out to investigate,
hauling into your clothes,
          just in case.
I watched you leave like a man
about to liberate
                    a nation.

On being a million miles from Christmas

The house was doused with heat. It fell
in wobbling waves from the corrugated roof,
bleaching the lawn white. I lived in small breaths,
held my limbs tight inside a Laura Ashley dress,
testing the sharp scrunch of grass underfoot.

Afternoons burned on the pool. Everywhere
the heavy pant of dogs, their sagging tongues
dripping thirst onto the lawn, their pelts heavy
with sun. At intervals they staggered to the pool
to lap the idle blue, then sank back down.

There was no wind to usher in a new season,
and end the long reign of light. I sucked an ice-
cube like a fraught dream of snow, the hard relief
from slurred heat, that came to nothing.

Admissions

(i)

Something dark and sobering crests
the bushes in the garden, the tattered
trees empty, and even the ladleful of light
down the far wall looks implausible.

At least I know I'm not God this time -
which is progress, I suppose, but instead
you're taciturn, suffering like an old man
confined to his house, remote and difficult.

Some days it has consoled to go out,
to unbolt the door to the ornamental world
and feel again the effort of true cold,
the sprawled lawn reckless with morning.

I have seen you hold out your hands
to the birds, coax your spit-softened butts
to their mouths, admonishing gently, as if
you fancied yourself St Francis of Assisi.

You can't bear how abandoned you are:
no more the secret voices whispering
God's prognosis, but the same old
prescribed silence. You miss the luxury

of prophesy, your wise and noisy body
passing clean through the public gaze.
You believe it a necessary disobedience
to the laws and artifice by which we live

so quietly. You want the clothes you wore
through the blood and smoke of your infamy,
jeans fought in and torn, that stink of fire.
And proudly, you lift your shirt to show me

the soft shock of a boot sole to your chest,
daubing your flesh still, your knuckles grazed
from where they pinned you to the ground:
I took on five men and defeated them. I won.

(ii)

You fall asleep in the bath and are declared 'unwakeable'.
                        It takes four men and swearwords
                to wrench you vertical
                        and even then you hang between them,
                        a dripping king,
                                        asleep.

You know the protocols of suffering:
                        today you're half-ashamed, half-
                proud, of how naked you have been.
                        You rouse the ward with your rendition of
'Always Look on the Bright Side of life', until
                the mute are whistling.
                        If I can just convince the doctors I know I'm ill,

                                        I'll be laughing

(iii)

This was not the man I knew
those formal mornings of our courtship -
all clean sheets and shy gratitude
for the night before.

And you were not the man who stood,
late on, in the late days of your shaking,
out in the road, the hall light shining
beautifully for no one.

Nor the man who battered doors
as though to reach a panicked child,
or the blood of the wood,
who would not come home.

But this was who I feared and felt
when I entered the long body of your life
with its lithium taint, the *soft, silver-white
metallic element* that held you
steady and compliant,
even as your hands were shaking.

Memorial Weekend

and pairs of sailors take the streets in their iconic whites,
outmoded heartthrobs, or boys absconded from school,

proud and vulnerable in their uniforms, they take turns
to smoke or talk on the phone while their side-kick

keeps watch on the horizon: the unwavering glass
and steel of these recklessly vertical buildings.

They move in perfect unison down the avenues,
their sailor collars lolloping in a diligent breeze,

conjuring the antique dazzle of the sea. Downtown
their flagrant whites like cowbells lure tough guys -

mid-darts – to bar doorways, who sneer as they pass:
they could have them for dinner. Their soft boys' hearts

seem unsalted, breakable, as they pose for photographs
outside FAO Schwartz, their hours ashore one long souvenir.

The Particulars

My mother forgets how to sleep. 5am
she is hoovering: the frenzy of a woman
who needs to sell a house – and fast.
Her mind's austere with cleaning fluid.

I ghost myself in doorways; enter only
to temper light rendered oddly in a room,
or shield curtains shameful with flowers.
Unseemly details we ushered into cupboards

or rammed in drawers. I tell viewers
how sorry we are to leave a house like this -
its banisters lambent with beeswax,
bedspreads that flinch beneath our touch;

fresh coffee wafts in across the glossy lake
of tabletop. Coats hunched on the newel post
are frogmarched to hooks behind the door,
where shoes line up in drill along the mat,

on standby for exodus. Everything has
a place, even us, even my father, who lurches
in his study - distressed - and begins to
talk in front of guests. A man at home

in his life, a man who climbed four flights
and reached his peak, then couldn't budge -
the mould of his body in the chair's leather;
just the gloat of light at his door's edge, or

the creak of his chair arching back in sleep.
Nights I stood on the stairs calling his supper
and waited – my face upturned to silence,
like weather, falling slowly from its source.

I think of arachnids under glass

the mechanics of love which move quietly
and freeze when observed.

An inordinate calm stirs
through the rooms and a song begins...

I would like to dance with you,
to do what we never did, now,

while it is still too late -

the sliding communion of hearts and eyes
in the lilac of all twilights.

Tell me what fool I am – my risen dresses,
the years it took me to prepare,

and my dread of the departure hour
when you slid away like water,

every touch insufferably lovely.

Dylan Thomas has his photograph taken

He is at most a torso, floating formal in a rising sea of
ivy, the graveyard's wrought iron bedsteads behind
him. *Neither a ghost nor a man,* he stands solemn in
his DJ and dicky bow, one hand in his pocket as
though fumbling for a ticket, the unwelcome lustre of
sunlight exposing the ends of his hair to a halo. His
mouth's remorseless. He has understood the decency
of the dead bowing out in their own good time,
giving up their long labour of attachment to the earth,
in their best suits and skirts, their Sunday shoes,
buffed to a sheen to catch God's eye. Elsewhere the
enterprise continues. Already he is worn in the
graveyard's afternoon, but the pardons and squalors
will go on for some time. He has not hit the biggest of
the biggies yet, but he is warm, *warm...*

Tableau

The cursive billow of tablecloth by a window,
the perfect pared bodies of salt and pepper,
stark on that bolt of cloth, immaculate in cream:
the tableau of a life I might have lived in.
Those things I said, I never meant them;
it's in the past and still the coldness, the heavy
hand on a leg, the quiet cups, they plague,
and won't give up their hold. *Can I just say?*

It seems it was darker in those days, though
all the lights were on, and every room illuminate
with feeling, as though made good by touch.
Times I'd watch you from the doorway, drowsy
but arousable in my underwear, some late o'clock,
the blood assumption thumping in the air between us
and the liability of a look; I could fix you a gaze
at the most superior point in the range - and you'd *flip.*